Mike Haskins has written a number of humour books including the bestselling joke collection *Man Walks into a Bar*. He has also written scripts for the likes of Steve Coogan, Simon Pegg, Milton Jones, Punt and Dennis, Smack the Pony and Smith and Jones.

WOW, I'M A GENIEOUS!!!!

Mike Haskins

CONSTABLE · LONDON

Constable & Robinson Ltd.
55–56 Russell Square
London WC1B 4HP
www.constablerobinson.com

First published in the UK by Constable,
an imprint of Constable & Robinson Ltd., 2014

A copy of the British Library Cataloguing in Publication
Data is available from the British Library

ISBN: 978-1-47211-101-2 (paperback)
ISBN: 978-1-47211-108-1 (ebook)

Printed and bound by CPI Group (UK) Ltd, Croydon, CR0 4YY

3 5 7 9 10 8 6 4 2

Introduction

Years ago, if you said or did something stupid or embarrassing, it would have remained relatively private and would soon have been forgotten.

Now, thanks to advances in technology, every cringe-making remark that we make online is not only preserved for the rest of eternity but also instantly available for the whole world to see!

In the old days, if we wanted to moan about the shortcomings of our boss we'd do it behind closed doors, but now we sound off in an email and get so carried away we don't realize we've hit 'reply all' before sending it. And, sod's law being what it is, the person we've been slagging off is right there at the top of the recipients list.

When we think we're doing a great service to mankind by writing a product review for something we've just bought online we forget that there's no spellchecker pointing out that 'satnav' does not have an 'h' in it or that Dolly Parton's surname does not start with an 'f'.

And that's quite apart from the myriad errors of grammar, punctuation and other sorts that litter our masterworks.

If we take to social networking we may forget that our 1,300 'friends' are not remotely interested in where exactly on our body we found an interesting new spot or how many Negroni cocktails we consume before breakfast. Our future employers, of course, may well be *very* interested several years down the line when we apply for a job – especially if it's with the police or the Church of England.

Then there are those innocent searches for information. When we ask a silly question, such as: 'What is the main ingredient for pumpkin soup?' or 'How did Fats Domino get his nickname?', we will be for ever remembered as 'that idiot' who posted the question on a website and ended up in a book such as this.

Luckily, we are not the only fools out there. How long is it since you had one of those emails from a multimillionaire asking you to look after a few million for him? Naturally, all you have to do is give him all your bank details, including your password, and Bob's your uncle – or he would be if he hadn't scarpered with all *your* cash.

But your suspicions would have been aroused by his curious name, 'King Sir Bountiful Smith III', or the fact that although he has singled you out as a trustee for his fortune he does not appear to know your name, but simply addresses you as 'Dear'.

You may have had an email purporting to be from your bank, asking for your 'parsword'. Apart from not being able to spell 'password' they also appear to be unable to spell the name of the bank they are writing from. Although educational standards may have slipped in recent years, you would imagine that genuine employees of Lloyds Bank would know that the name begins with two 'l's.

Perhaps it's comforting to know that whatever stupid thing you may have said online has been topped by something far worse. If ignorance is bliss, some of these people must be in a permanent state of delirious ecstasy.

So join us as we find the people who put the twit in Twitter and the mess in instant message.

George Orwell was wrong: Big Brother isn't watching you but, thanks to the Internet, everybody else in the world is!

Stupid Questions and Stupid Answers

We've all asked some daft questions in our time, haven't we? Whether it's seeking directions to a road we're already in, or enquiring after the health of someone who is at the time ill in hospital, or perhaps musing on who put the bomp in the bomp ah bomp bah bomp.

But the Internet has taken stupid questions to a whole new level. While at one time we would only have been thought stupid by the handful of people who heard us ask why you never hear West Indians speak Jamaican, now it is possible to be ridiculed by half the population of the world.

If you manage to come out with something spectacularly stupid you may even find that it's 'gone viral'. Meaning, of course, that every person who sees your stupid comment will pass it on to ten friends, who will in turn each send it to ten friends, and so on until very soon you are the laughing stock of the entire planet!

And it's not just daft questions you have to worry about, it's daft answers too. When somebody looking for investment advice asks if anyone can recommend the best bond and you say, 'Well, Sean Connery for the action but Roger Moore for the humour', the world will have you marked down as a bit of a plonker – especially if you are employed as a financial adviser at the time.

But, however spectacularly you mess up, there will be someone else who has done it ten times worse. And perhaps that's the beauty of the Internet and its exposure of the dotty, daft or demented; you will realize that you are not the most stupid person in the world. There are dozens, perhaps thousands, or even millions, of people out there who make you look like a cross between Albert Einstein and Shakespeare.

So, get that stupidometer ready . . .!

Stupid Questions and Stupid Answers: Science and Technology

What percentage of water is celery?

They told us at school that celery basically has nothing in it and really it's just all water. So exactly what percentage of water is celery?

How do i turn my computer monitor into a mirror?

i want to turn my computer monitor so when it comes on the screen is like a mirror. does anyone know if you can do that? i have tried just scanning a mirror but that doesn't work.

How does anyone know the names of dinosaurs?

There was no people alive when dinosaurs were around. so how did anyone ever find out what they were called?

Can an electric fan blow the particles from a wireless signal?

I'm having trouble with the connection in my room and it's quite a big fan so I'm wondering if it's blown away all the wireless stuff in the air.

Where can you buy photosynthesis?

I am growing some seeds in my bedroom and my dad says i need to get some photosynthesis coz my plant only has 2 leaves on it. but where can I buy photosynthesis? and how much does it cost (for each photosynthesi)?

What's the big deal with global warming?

If the temperature goes up can't we just wear less clothes and maybe turn on the air conditioning if it gets relly bad?

What was on the Internet before it was discovered?

What sorts of websites did it have when it was discovered?

If the earth is really 4 billion years old, why is it still only the year 2013?

Was oxygen really only discovered in 1783? And if so what the hell were people breathing before that?

What are we going to do to get ice after global warming?
Will we have to invent something else to make our drinks cold?

How many horizons are there?

If we're 98% water why do we need to drink anything?

How can a temperature be minus anything? If it's minus it doesn't exist does it?

Does anyone know if looking at pictures of the sun will damage my eyes?

Why doesn't the Earth just like fall down?

How do they know the sun is 93 million miles away – has anyone ever actually measured it?

What does light years mean? Are they like the opposite of heavy years?

Dwayne J:

Hey! How come there's no air conditioning App on the iPhone?!

Perez T:

Sure there's a fan app on the iPhone, dumbass! This is how it works:

1. Take your iPhone in one hand;
2. Shake it back and forth as fast as possible in front of your face;
3. Enjoy cool refreshing breeze.

Stupid Questions and Stupid Answers: Animals

Who first invented the idea of milking cows for milk?

I'm guessing the guy involved must have been some kind of cow abuser.

Could I have killed my cat by farting on it?

Or was it just the fact that I sat on it?

Is there something wrong with me if I keep watching my dog licking his willy?

It's not like it gets me excited or anything but yesterday I watched him licking his willy for over ten minutes. Then my mum came in and told him off and then she gave me a look and I felt a little bit guilty.

Why do crocodiles walk so gayly?

What is with crocodiles? Why do they walk like they just got their nails done or something.

I don't get that kids game what's the time mr wolf?

I mean like why would a wolf no the time anyways?

Did anyone else see a REAL dinosaur in the Inverary area last night . . .?

I was out in the woods. It was quiet. I couldn't see anyone around because it was dark. Then suddenly there was a big ROARR and I caught a glimpse of what I can only describe as an actual large live dinosaur running back across the A819. I think it might have been heading towards the golf club. I repeat, this was A GENUINE, LIVING dinosaur and I had not had that much to drink. It was not an enormous brontesaurus or a tyrannosaurus or anything like that. But it was about 6 foot tall and grey coloured. But then it was dark. And it had spikes all down its neck to its tail. It disappeared into the bushes and I ran home because I had just seen a dinosaur. So do dinosaurs still exist in places???? PLEASE TELL ME I NEED TO KNOW!

PS:

This is a genuine question, and I am definitely telling the truth. I took a photo on my phone but it is all black cos it was dark.

Did we have nocturnal animals before there was street lighting?

How does it happen that the holes in a cats fur are always exactly in the right place for their eyes?

They say there's no such thing as a bad dog, just a bad owner so how does the owner get bad?

Are tortoises able to leave their shells and walk round on their own?

Do ants have dicks?

Is it wrong if your cat looks at you when you have no clothes on and you are a girl and your cat is a boy?

How do reptiles know when they're full?

Did anyone else know that a puma is not just a shoe brand but an actual animal?? I am stunned.

Is it possible to tell if a movie doesn't use real dinosaurs?

I am filling in my tax return. Is there any way I can claim my cat as a co dependent? THIS IS A SERIOUS QUESTION!

What's the best way to free your dog's testicles if they get caught in a couple of mouse traps?

I have a Rottweiler called Geordie and sometimes he likes to sleep in the cellar. I put a couple of mouse traps down there last week. I didn't think these would be dangerous to the dog. But last night he must have sat on two of the traps because they've snapped on his nut sac. He's got a pair of mouse traps clanking around between his legs like a pair of maracas. He is quite a young dog and he has quite large testicles about the size of billiard balls. He is ok but he is not very happy just now. The problem is he won't let me get near enough to release his scrotum. I feel too embarrassed to take him to the vet with those traps clapping together as he walks and him yowling along. What should I do? If I had taken him to the vet to get him done the other week this would never have happened.

Stupid Questions and Stupid Answers: Health

How many calories are there in a bogey?

I've just eaten one but I'm supposed to be on a diet.

Someone told me toothpaste burns you if you put it on the end of your willy.

Is there any way I can check if this is true?

Is it possible to get high from sniffing Dr Pepper?

I heard you can get high from sniffing coke. I've only got Dr Pepper in the fridge. Does anyone know if that works as well?

Can someone advise what is the best way to lose weight without moving?

I do not like moving. Also I am allergic to the sun.

My sister says putting on lipstick makes your boobs grow bigger. Is that really true?

I've tried it and it doesn't seem to work. Or is it cos I need to put it on my boobs?

If a person swallows too much of their own saliva, could they eventually drown?

Which bits of me is it legal for my sister to massage?

Is rubbing your stomach a good way to lose weight?

Could I have little flies coming out of me in my wee?

Whenever I go for a wee I notice there is a little fly floating in the toilet water afterwards. I'm certain it wasn't there before I weed. Have I got flies inside me somewhere?

Is it ok for my wife to eat her own placenta if she is a vegetarian?

I have read it is very healthy if you eat your placenta after you have given birth. the thing is my wife and I are very strict vegetarians. so we are not sure what the official position is. obviously my wife's placenta is made of meat. so can she eat it and still be a vegetarian?

How can I stop myself chewing the end of my penis all the time?

I meant to ask how can I stop myself chewing the end of my pen. Can someone advise how I can amend my original question? Quickly please!

How can I get a plaster cast on my wrist?

I told everyone at school I broke my wrist. But I haven't really. Now I've got to go to school and everyone will see I haven't broke my wrist. Where can I get a plaster cast to put on my wrist to make it look broke? Or is the best thing to actually break it?

How can I stop my skin going wrinkly and coming off?

I am worried about my skin. You know how it goes all wrinkly if you go in water for too long? Some friends want me to go to their house and spend all day in their swimming pool. Is my skin going to just crumple up completely and start coming off? How many hours does this take to happen?

What's the best thing to do if you wake up and found your rear is completely plugged up?

I've tried everything. Yawning, taking a deep breath, blowing my nose. Just can't unblock it.

Stupid Questions and Stupid Answers: The World and Its People

Does anyone know if it rains in Australia?

i was arguing about this with my friend. my friend says that it rains in australia. but that can't be right can it because obviously the rain falls to the top of the earth but australia is at the bottom so the rain wouldn't fall to earth it would fall into space.

Does anyone know what a person from London is called?

Best answer: My neighbour is from London. He is called Kevin.

Where did black people originally come from?

Best answer: Africa

Answer: No it wasn't, you dumb s***. They came from Egypt.

Is it true that Chinese people don't need to go to the toilet?

How deep is the specific ocean?

Apart from Christianity which other religions celebrate Christmas?

Where about's in africa is india?

Can Siamese twins have sex with each other?

Is London England named after London Kentucky?

What is the capital of the South Pole and who is the current president?

How do people know about things that happened in history if they weren't actually there to see them at the time?

Is the Taj Mahal in India the head quarters of all the Indian restaurants round the world that are called the Taj Mahal?

Is it true that the French don't use toilet paper because they say it isn't part of their culture? Or was my dad lying?

What is a non-racist way to refer to Siamese twins?

Macie L:
How did people find their way round before google maps was invented?
Chris H:
They used maps.
Macie L:
No!!!!! Pay attention, asshole!!!! I said before google maps!!!!

Stupid Questions and Stupid Answers: People

Does anyone know Obama's last name?

Is stevie wonder really still blind?

Is adolf hitler the same person as hitler?

Is Elvis Presley a real person or was he just a character in a film?

Is the Dalai Lama an actual lama?

Is Michael Jackson genuinely dead or is it just a publicity stunt?

Who is the musician called 'Feat' and how does he get to appear on so many records?

How does the pope keep control of his pope mobile when he is driving it along and he is standing up in the back waving to everyone?
Best answer: It is a miracle.

What is the name of the man who painted the Mona Lisa?
Best answer: Leonardo di Caprio.

Does Father Christmas really exist or have my mummy and daddy been lying to me my entire life?

What is the name of the guy who invented fashion?

Stupid Questions and Stupid Answers:
The Great Questions of Life

Do midgets have night vision?

a friend of mine says that midgets have got night vision. i wasn't sure if that was right. i know a little person who is at my school tho. so i phoned him up and i asked him but he didn't say anything. he just hanged up the phone. this has left me very confused. does anyone know for certain if midgets do have night vision?

OK men, stick close to Private Smith he has night vision

How do I get YouTube to come and film me?

I have phoned YouTube and written to them over and over but they never reply. I guess they're busy but how do I get them to come and put me in one of their videos? I can do some real funny stuff but I can't get them to come.

How can I ask a question on this online message board?

Best answer: Er, you just did!

Is it true that you can get giant midgets?

If a person owns a piece of land, do they own it right through to the middle of the earth?

My council tax is the same as next door's so how come my gas bill is higher?

Does vodka have alcohol in it or does alcohol have vodka in it?

Why do lifts have a button for the floor that you're already on – you're already there! Duh!

Why do they put seeds in grapes?

Does anyone know what song it is that goes: Hm Hm
Hm Hm Hm Hm Hm Hm Hm . . .

It has some music in the background and starts –
Hm Hm Hm Hm Hm. And then it goes higher pitched
– Hm Hm Hm Hm Hm Hm. Then it is the same as at
the beginning – Hm Hm Hm Hm Hm Hm. Actually it
might be – HmmHmHmHmmHmmmm.

I think it is a woman going Hm Hm Hm Hm.

What is the name of this song?

Is it true that everyone has a gardian angle?

How can I become a train?

Is there a magic spell to turn you into a fairy that really
works?

Just wondering – did someone come up with 911 for the
police number because of 9/11?

Stupid Questions and Stupid Answers: Relationships and Sex

How many periods do you have to miss before you know you're pregnant?

Best answer: nine.

Can you tell your husband has been cheating on you by the smell he makes when he farts?

I think you can. He tells me he is working late but when he gets home and farts there is a bit of a smell of someone else's perfume.

Can a man be arrested for indecently exposing himself if he is in his own house?

Can a man be arrested for indecent exposure if he is on his own in his house watching the television and he is naked? Does it make any difference if the curtains are open?

If a vagina isn't used will it eventualy close up and heal over?

Can you get pregnant by oral sex – like if you accidentally swallow or something?

Can someone tell me how to get twins? Is it true I need to have sex with two different guys?

Can sex be good if you don't have an organism?

Is it true you won't get pregnant if you use a tampon?

How does poo and pee and periods all come out of the same hole?

Does your dog know what you are doing when you masturbate in front of him? I am asking on behalf of a friend who needs to know.

I just drank a large cold glass of cola but afterwads it made me MORE thirsty. Does this mean I cud be pregnint?

Best answer: Why would you think this means that you'd be pregnant? I'm pretty sure wanting seconds of fizzy drink is not a symptom of pregnancy.

I just noticed on my wife's facebook page she has changed her status from 'married' to 'widowed'. What does this mean?

Best answer: It means you should be seriously worried.

Answer: Sleep well, brother!

What do prostitutes wear during the winter?

What do they put on to make themselves look all prostitutey when it's freezing cold outside? Cos if you wore a jumper and a big coat people wouldn't be able to tell you were a prostitute. Or do they just have to do some other kind of job in the winter?

Why has my brother not got his first period yet?

I'm twelve and have had mine but my brother is sixteen and has had nothing? Is it cos he is a boy and so it takes longer?

Best answer: Yes, it is because he is a boy. It takes longer for boys.

Why don't hetrosexuals stop making homosexuals?

All homesexuals come from two hetrosexuals. A mother heterosexual and a father heterosexual. That is a fact. So why do hetrosexuals keep making homesexuals? Why don't they just stop this thing right now?

Do any of you people know any Sagitariuses?

What are they like? Do they suck? I need to know cos if they are I am going to tell hubby access is denied this month so I don't end up having one.

Am I a lesbian?

I saw this really cute guy but after we got talking I realized it was a really ugly girl. Does this mean I am a lesbian?

How can I stop my penis glowing in the dark?

Some friends were messing about at a music festival last weekend and they poured a broken glowstick into my underpants. Now my penis is covered in glowstick juice. Now my dick is really itchy and it glows in the dark. Does anyone know how long this will last?

Is it true if you put deodorant on your penis it stops you making sperm?

Best answer: No, but your babies will smell lovely and will never sweat.

Answer: If you put enough on it might stop it getting out.

What happens if you die when you've got an erection?
Does it go away or is it stuck like that forever?

Best answer: Your dick will be stuck like that forever. Everyone at your funeral is going to be wondering why the lid of your coffin won't close properly.

Answer: Don't worry. The undertaker can use it to hold the lid of the coffin open during viewings.

If you have run out of condoms, is it ok to snip off the fingers from a household rubber glove and use those instead?

This girl I know leaves tomorrow and I cant think of anything else in the flat I have left for contraception. Please reply by three o'clock so I can make a decision. I'll let you all know if it worked ok. We have to use something in case she gets pregnant. She can't take the pill any more because it was effecting her driving.

Update: Hurry up, guys! I've got blue balls a go go here!

Update: OK, I'm just going to have to give it a try and hope for the best! Will report back later!

Update: Went well. We snipped up a rubber glove and stretched it out. It was ok but a bit tight and it stung a bit cos I had used it for cleaning the sink and then it came off inside her. No worries tho cos eventualy she managed to get it out but now she's a bit mad cos that was our only form of contraception. Do you think she will be pregnant?

Why don't girls like to have sex during their periods?

You'd think it would might help make them feel better.

How many bones does the male penis contain?

And does it contain more bones when it gets big?

If I take a photo of my own penis am I breaking the law?

I am only sixteen. Will I be committing child sex abuse on myself?

Will I understand the plot of *Lesbian Cheerleaders Anal Intrusion 3*?

I just bought a DVD called *Lesbian Cheerleaders Anal Intrusion 3*. Does anyone know what happened in parts 1 & 2. I am worried I am not going to be able to pick up the story?

How do you get an orgasm from a tampon?

Best answer: It depends. Are you a man or a lady?

If you have sex and you are pregnant can having sex get the baby pregnant too?

What I mean is like if there is a baby up there already and some of the sperm gets up there some of that sperm must be able to get into the baby too, right? So what I want to know is can the baby get pregnant? Girls are getting pregnant younger and younger these days so I am worried.

My friend told me you don't have to use a condom with women from Thailand because they cannot get pregnant?

Best answer: Yes, it is true – but it is because they are not really women.

My son is not gay. However he has a very good friend who is a man. They spend all their time together and go out together all the time. The other day I found them in my son's room having sex. Does this definitely mean my son's friend is gay?

Best answer: It means they're both gay, you asshole!

My girlfriend says when she goes with other boys they always use a comdom. So she says it is not realy cheatin. Also she says it's usualy pretty quick. Is it cheatin tho?

Best answer: Comdom or no comdom, it is cheating. Dump her now!

How can you tell if someone is a boy or a girl?

Like if someone you know is going out with someone but you are not sure if it is a boyfriend or a girlfriend cos they don't quite look like either a boy or a girl and you can't tell from their clothes or anything. And their name is Toni but you've never seen it written down so it might be Tony. How can I tell? And does this mean I could be gay and not know it?

How do I take off my mother's bra?

Help! Someone tell me quick! She's going to be home in five minutes!

What does it mean if someone comes up to you every day and says woof?

Best answer: It means they are a dog.

Answer: If you are worried about it you could always ring canine canine canine.

Stupid Questions and Stupid Answers: Family Matters

How can I get my mum and dad to get a divorce?

All my friends' mums and dads are divorced. Why aren't mine? If they were I'd get loads more presents and get taken out to great places at the weekend. My mum and dad aren't even thinking of getting divorced? How did I make them? They don't even have sex or anything any more so what's the point?

Do I need to break it to my mum and dad that I am adopted?

I don't look like them. I don't get on with them. I don't like them. I think I need to tell them straight – I must have been adopted.

Does anyone know which rapper uses the least bad language?

My son is fifteen and he likes rap music. I do not mind my son listening to rap music but the amount of swearing in some of the rap numbers concerns me. I do not want him to pick up bad habits so I would be grateful if anyone could supply me with a list of the names of rap musicians who do not swear or who use only very mild language.

Helen B:

What should I do? I am worried about my son. He is sixteen years old and I am concerned that he may have a girlfriend that he hasn't told myself or his father about. We have noticed that he has become quite secretive of late. He will not come with us to church and today I have found hidden under his bed a magazine full of pictures of naked men. There is clearly only one explanation. He has got himself a girlfriend who has brought these pictures into our house.

PS: He is not homosexual or anything like that. He has been taught in church, at home and at school that such things are an abhorrence to the Lord. I am however concerned that he may get his secret girlfriend pregnant as she is so clearly filled with lust for naked men.

People Who Really Don't Deserve Our Money

It's bad enough being conned out of your hard-earned cash by clever crooks, but when someone with an IQ of six and a half legs it with your loot it's not just aggravating, it's pretty embarrassing too.

Imagine being stopped in the street by a dodgy-looking character in a dirty mac and told in broken English that he's the managing director of Barclays Bank and can you please give him all your personal details including your online banking password and user name.

Naturally you would do so immediately. But only if you are as daft as he thinks you are, which, of course, you're not.

Online scams are the digital equivalent of the man in the dirty mac, but many people still fall for them.

Whether it's Nigerian potentates who have so much money they need you to look after a few million for them, or people who have won the lottery and want to share it with you, or someone who has just been mugged in some far-flung place and needs urgent funds, the first person they think of is little ol' you!

As things stand at the moment, the CEOs of most major corporations can more or less spell, so anyone who addresses you as 'Dear costumer' should arouse your suspicions immediately.

The way educational standards are going though, this may not be a foolproof method of detection for much longer.

Good Day!

I am the manager of bills and exchange at the foriegn remittance department of the (ABN AMRO BANK AMSTERDAM). I am writting you this letter to ask for your support and co-operation to carry out this transaction. We discovered some abandoned sum $15,500,000 (FIFTEEN MILLION, FIVE HUNDRED THOUSAND U.S DOLLAR) in an account that belongs to one of our foriegn customer who died along-side his entire family in march this year in a terrorist train bomb blast in Spain some few months ago. Since this development, we have advertised for his next of kin or any close relation to come forward to claim this money, but nobody came yet to apply for the claim.

Please contact me even if you are not intrested in my proposal to you to enable us scout for another partner in the event of non-interest on your part. Thanks for your co-operation

Mr Piet Van Jan

—m—

FROM ME ERIC H MILLER ERIC

I am. Eric miller and I am British soldier attached to UN peacekeeping force in Iraq. As you may know there are several cases of insurgent attacks and suicde bombings going on here. We have managed to move funds belonging to some demised persons who were attacked and killed through these attacks. The total amount is US$15 million dollars in cash. We want to move this money to you . . .

PLEASE TREAT THIS PROPOSAL AS TOP SECRET

Great news dear, I've transferred all our savings to a chap in Africa who will double them immediately

Dear Friend,

I know that this message will come to you as a surprise.
I AM A SECRETARY OF FOREIGN REMITTANCE
DIRECTOR BOA BANK HERE IN OUAGADOUGOU
BURKINA FASO. I Hope that you will not expose or
betray this trust and confident that i am about to repose
on you for the mutual benefit of our both families.

I need your urgent assistance in transferring the sum of
($7.6)million to your account within 14 banking days. This
money has been dormant for years in our Bank without
claim. I want the bank to release the money to you as the
nearest person to our deceased customer, the owner of
the account died along with his supposed next of kin in an
air crash since July 31st 2000 . . .

Best Regard.
ALIHU UMAR

—⁂—

From: your good friend

am in Limassol, Cyprus at the moment, I am here for a conference. I was sitting outside a cafe when gypsies on motor bikes rode by and cut through my bag with knife and rode off immediately. I had all my money, cards and other personal effects in the bag.

I have been trying to sort things out with the necessary authorities and consulate, I need some financial assistance from you.

Let me know if you can be of any help.

—⁓—

ATTENTION DEAR SIR OR MADAM,
THE MANAGEMENT OF CENTRAL BANK OF
NIGERIA PLC, WISHES TO INFORM YOU THAT WE
ARE IN RECEIPT OF YOUR CONFIRMED BANK
DRAFT CHEQUE ISSUED IN YOUR FAVOUR WITH
CASH AMOUNT OF ONE MILLION FIVE HUNDRED
US DOLLARS, FROM YOUR AGENT AND HE TOLD
US TO ARRANGE YOUR PAYMENT TO BE
AVAILABLE BY WESTERN UNION DUE TO THE

FACT THAT YOU CAN NOT BE ABLE TO CASH THE TOTAL $1.5MILLION CHEQUE,

(URGENT BUSINESS ASSISTANCE STRICTLY CONFIDENTIAL)

COMPLIMENTS OF THE SEASON

Good Day,

I am a Senior Auditor working with a Bank here in Malaysia, I have a deal of $9.7m are you in interest to receive this fund into your Bank Account or your open up a new Bank Account to receive the usd$9.7m and we share 50/50% after you have receive sum into your bank account.

The $9.7m left behind by a late customer, a Iraq citizen Mr Mohamat H Ammar who died with his entire family in Iraq War before it is declared unserviceable by my Bank.

Firstly, I will like to clearly make you understand, that . . .

Yours Sincerely.

Mr Savior P.winna

Dear Partner

PRIVATE AND CONFIDENTIAL

My name is Owen Clarke, I am the credit manager in a bank here in the West Africa. I am contacting you of a business transfer, of a huge sum of money from a deceased account. Though I know that a transaction of this magnitude will make any one apprehensive and worried, but I am assuring you that everything has been well taken care off, and all will be well at the end of the day. I decided to contact you due to the urgency of this transaction. To ease your apprehension, I got your contact from the British chambers of commerce and industry, foreign trade division . . .

—◊◊◊—

Postings from the Social Network

Talking in textspeak was always going to lead to confusion. While normal conversation is mercifully free of this ur-language most of the time, the online social network is full of conversations that would have been incomprehensible even a decade ago.

And that's even before you add in the textspeak!

Who was it who once said of somebody, 'He's got nothing to say, but he will insist on saying it'? Whoever it was could have had certain social networkers in mind.

The worrying thing is that when people write something, they've presumably thought about it first before putting fingers to keyboard – or maybe they haven't. It could explain some of the strange ramblings out there.

Somebody once said that if you gave a thousand monkeys a thousand typewriters and let them type for a thousand years they would eventually come up with the complete works of Shakespeare. Hey, world, we're still waiting for those Bard-like gems!

And then there's the question of self-censorship. Most of us have a little voice in the back of our mind saying, 'Er, you can't really say that', or 'On second thoughts, I'd better tone that down a bit', or 'If I write that, Beyoncé/Jeffrey Archer/Sir Mick Jagger might sue me for libel.'

Sadly, that doesn't always seem to be the case and some people's internal little angels are overruled by their devilish counterparts, who write the first thing that comes into their heads. Luckily for us, as it happens – or we wouldn't have this chapter.

Postings from the Social Network: Reaching Out to All Nations

Grayson W:
[immediately after the Japanese tsunami of 2011]
i don't believe there was no damn tsunami. it's just the japs trying to trick us. i just went on google streetview. everything still looks fine over there as far as i can see.

Sarah:

They just announced on the news that the US is bombing Labia.

Col:

Woah! Bombing Labia! That sounds damn painful!!

Tom:

My God! How much of a pounding can Labia take?

Bill:

Can't they ever leave female anatomy in peace?

Rog:

I love Labia. It's such a beautiful, hidden, densely forested area.

Lenny:

I am proud to be an American so it makes me mad when foreigners say America is the stupidest country in the world. Bullshit! In my opinion Europe is the stupidest country in the world.

Alfonso:

I think those damn A-rabs are barbarans. How can they go round beheading people like that? Why can't they do like civilised nations and use the electric chair?

Doug:

I have noticed on the news every time you see a picture taken in the Middle East there is always a crowd of people. Don't these people have to go to work?

Trevor:

Hurricanes are nothing but a bit of rain and wind. And yet the Yanks bleat on about them endlessly. Why do they always have to make such a big deal out of everything?

Frank:

Australia wants to get rid of Her Majesty? Well, what do you expect from an ex-colony populated entirely by criminals and prostitutes?

Bill:

In my opinion Liverpool is the capital city for scumbags, thieves, trouble makers and benefit scroungers. Anyone from Liverpool who makes any money uses it to get out and live somewhere – anywhere – else, e.g. Cilla, The Beatles, Jimmy Tarbuck.

Postings from the Social Network: Obituary Corner

Shaz:

Rip Bob Marley . . . No idea you weren't still alive.

Click 'like' to pay your respects:

Bee Gees co-founder Robin Gibb is dead aged sixty-two.

5,146 people like this.

Fergy:

Rip Larry Hagman – to be honest I thought you were already dead. Maybe you came back and died again. In which case RIP squared.

Hank:

So sad how Michael Jackson died from Cadillac arrest man RIP.

Ronni:

Whitny Houston – so sad you are gone altho I never rely liked your records and thoght you were a terible example to young peeple.

Fats:

Micheal Jackson RIP – this is a BIG mistake for sumone. you should not have died, Michael. sumone is gonna get their ass sued for this!! big time!!!!

Joaquin:

What a disgrace! Lance Armstrong – the first astronaut on the moon has now admitted he used steroids and the like to get there. All the text books will have to be re-written.

Keenan:

You have exceeded all previous standards of human stupidity. You're thinking of Neil Armstrong! And what's more the guy has died.

Joaquin:

Congratulations! You have now demonstrated to the entire world exactly how stupid YOU are. Haven't you seen the news? The guy's name is LANCE Armstrong. He was on Oprah being interviewed. Now he has died. Do not leave comments on here unless you know WHAT THE HELL you are talking about!

Travis Q:

steve jobs, RIP.

Jermayne H:

who's steve jobs?

Travis Q:

steve jobs is the guy who invented the iPad, the iPod, the iPhone and a whole bunch of other computer stuff. Basically he is this generation's Albert Einstein.

Jermayne H:

albert einstien?!?! nah that sucker invented electricity no one can touch that shit!

Ray R:

erm, wasn't it Benjamin Franklin who invented electricity?

Jermayne H:

Lol! ok what did albert do?

Ray R:

Gravity.

Jermayne H:

u c! albert einstien invented gravity, benjamin franklin invented electricity, steve watsisname ain't even on the same level as them other suckers. w/o gravity n electricity we wud be useless an jus be floatin in outer space with computers we cant plug in. lol

Postings from the Social Network: Medical Matters

Deeta:

OMG. Girl with diabetees, the contagious kind, coughed on me at school today.

Elena:

Its not diabetees. U r thinkin of herpatitus. diabetees isn't usualy contagious.

Brent:

Both of you are simply retarded.

Leo:
Downer, man! My gran had her brain tumur taken out las night. Now she is in a comma.

Javine:
My momma was lactoast & tolerant. Dos that meen I cud be too?

Jake G:
Downer, man. My grandma's been to see the doctor and he's told her he's pretty sure she has die of beaties.

Barry:
That Zoe Saldana is nice lookin but I think she needs to eat sumthin. She looks anne or resick!

Reeta L:
ansomnia sucks.

Bennett:
It's called Insomnia, if you can't f***ing spell it you don't have it, you're probably doing something stupid and don't want to sleep or you just want to be a dumb c**t.

Angie P:

They say every kiss begins with a 'K'. Yeah well, so does klamidia.

Dominic:

I do not want to donate my organs after I die – I do not want my liver going to an alcoholic, my kidneys to a drug addict and my eyes to a paedophile.

Cliff H:

Read in the news some guy has been diagnosed with breast cancer! Surely's the guy's GP should be struck off! What kind of clown is this to come up with that kind of diagnosis? I'm not a doctor but even I know men do not have breasts! Sack the guy!!!

Postings from the Social Network: Relationships

Cynthia A:

Everyone's always saying 'long distance relationships never work'. Oh really? I have been with my amazing boyfriend over two years now. And guess what! He lives a couple of miles away! Long distance relationships never work? I say, 'Hey! Don't knock it till you try it!'

Mandy:

I am a good person I dont know why people cant see it. I slept with one of my friends husbands well technical shes not realy my friend I just use to work with her and was friends with him more than I was with her. And there having problems in there marriage anyways so realy I was doing both of them a fav. Now I'm going to go and have some more drinks to celebrate what a nice caring person I am.

Ed:

You are literally too stupid to insult.

Vincent:

If a girl has sex with a load of different guys then people call her a slut. But if a guy has sex with a load of different guys then he gets a fancy medical name ie he is a homosexual. No-one else see the double standards going on?

Troy:

Gentlemen, when I had sex last night it was as glorious as being in the final of the 100 metres at the Olympics

Gus:

Ok. So you mean it was all over in under ten seconds

Don:

No he means it was him, eight black guys and someone holding a gun.

Chantelle (girlfriend):

Derek, I wan u to no u r a small man in evry way. U do not no how to treat a lady n u jus f*** anything that walks. Tht is y u will never get me back. Also ur dick is crooked! Ther! Now evryone nos! Derek's dick is crooked!

Derek (boyfriend):

I don remember u complaining it was crooked when I wuz f***in u. Le me tel u I'm f***ing glad u dumped me, yo bitch. U saved me the truble of dumping ur ass. But it's low for u to go online and tell everyone in the world bout my dick on this shit! F*** u! Get this shit off line now, bitch!

Cynthia (Derek's mum):

Chantelle, I am sorry to interrupt this conversation but please would you delete your post about Derek's pee pee. He has been very upset the last few days. He cannot help the way he is and you should not make fun of him because of it. His father is not well endowed either but I would never make fun of him or tell everyone on the Internet.

Brenda:

I just get a load of ugly ass guys coming after me all the time. What's that all about? Ugly ass guys should go after the ugly ass girls. The hot good looking guys should go after the babes. Why isn't that obvious to everyone? Why do the ugly ass guys come after me?

Tigga:

Because you are one of the ugly ass girls. It is obvious to everyone.

Bob:

Do young ladies no longer bother trying to make themselves look attractive? It was all so different before our English roses ladies were 'liberated' by the femi-nazi equality brigade

Postings from the Social Network: Mathematical Conundra

Nige:

Can someone convert 1 minute 43.13 sec into seconds for me please.

Brendan:

Just add 60 seconds on? 103.13 I think.

Nige:

I'm confused. What do I add the 60 to?

Toots:

hey! i have just calculated that if i could only save £38 every week, i would have a million in less than 3 years! sounds like a plan to me!

Ron F:

So Lotto jackpot = $640 Million. Population of the USA = 300 million. So why not just give everyone 2.13 Million and call it a day!

Terri:

5 ft 9 is bigger than 5 ft 11 right. it always goes 8, 9, 10 so it must be like 5 ft 9 and then after that it's 6 ft. U cudnt go 5 ft 10, 5 ft 11, 6 ft. that wud make no sense at all. So that is why I reckon 5 ft 9 must be taller than 5 foot 11.

Postings from the Social Network:
Family Matters

Todd (son):

Thirty years old today. Jeez that sucks

Melissa (mum):

Happy birthday to my sweet little boy!!!!!!!!!!!

Todd:

Oh mum!

Melissa:

Thirty years ago today just after 12:05 pm you popped out of my va-jay-jay!!!!!!!

Todd:

You just had to tell everyone.

Deirdre L:

I have got a great name for my new daughter. Rainbow Trout. Isn't that beautiful? Does everyone think that is a great name?

Craig K:

For a fish, yes, it's fantastic. If though your daughter turns out to be human, it's possibly less good.

Jason:

I had a word with my five-year-old kid and told him there is no Father Christmas. It's me that leaves presents for him. I'm not going to let some fat old sod with a beard take credit for all my hard work. Especially not when the lazy bastard only works one day a year.

Brian (dad):

For the last time stop, will you treating me like I'm some sort of taxi driver! From now on if you want me to pick you up or take you anywhere, you have to start paying me!!!!

Kristi (daughter):

Dad, that will literally make you a taxi driver.

Gus P:

Shit man! What is this pic you just posted? It's all slime and shit all over it. Totally gross not cool at all. An instant delete. What is it?

Ben M:

It's an ultrasound pic of my unborn child.

Postings from the Social Network: Thank You for Sharing

Oliver:

I call Santa Claus Satan claus for at the pagan midwinter festival he comes with gifts. He slithers into children's houses. They celebrate by hanging effigies from the branches of a tree. Mistletoe adorns the rooms. A pagan fertility symbol as Satan Claus comes to deflower the children. He has laid low mankind with the gifts of avarice of Mammon. Prometheus, the god who gave human kind the gift of fire. He is the light bearer known to men as Lucifer. Behold Father Christmas.

Nathan:

I say all people are basically disgusting, vile hypocrites. And I refuse to leave my organs to them. I cannot bear to think of my kidneys vitals being used to save the life of any one of the scum of so called humanity today. Especially those who look at pornography of any kind but especially that with children (and that seems to be all of it), drug addict celebrities, the greedy pig bankers. ALL OF YOU!

Tim L:

Just saw the news. A beautiful girl gone missing. That's never going to turn out well. If she was ugly she'd probably have just run away. In which case there might have been some hope.

Josh P:

The best thing that could happen this year in my humble opinion – an asteroid will strike and cleanse the planet of the parasite we know as humankind.

Georgie:

Saw on the news ther is an asteroid comin cros space towards us. Jus try it, asteroid! C'mon! Give it yo best shot! Here I am waitin for ya! See! Nuthin! I'll be long dead for any asteroid hits me. Wish I cud see it tho. I hope it lands smack in the middle of Arab land and do us all a favour.

Ralph:

I watched the Jonathan Ross programme on television last night. I was extremely offended. I had to watch the programme all the way to the end to find out just how offensive it was.

Nico:

I think I'm being over-dramatic but as far as concerned *The X Factor* represents the end of Western civilisation as we know it

Max:

Just watching *Britain's Got Talent*. In my opinion it should be called Britain's got chavs.

Lucas G:

I consider myself quite liberal in my views but I think all benefit cheats should be taken out and shot in front of their children.

Danni:

None of us should eat or wear animals. Animals are our friends. We should not eat our friends.

Freddie:

I know three of ur friends who have eaten u.

Jenny J:

I think horse racing is disgusting and cruel.

Phil N:

I think your face is disgusting and cruel.

Andy is desperate for a huge poo.

227 people like this.

Postings from the Social Network: Pure Genieous

Cindy:

Wow! Just five weeks now till I get married in Hawaii!

Tiggy:

Wooo! Congratulations! So exactly when and where are you getting married?

Maesie P:

I am sorry but I am not going to apologise for who I am.

Chris N:

I'm sorry but did you just apologise for not apologising for who you are?

Babs:

Just bought some shoes online. Then when asked to pay I tried putting my credit card in the cd rom. Well, what the hell was I supposed to do!?! I wanted to see if the computer would read it. But now it's stuck. How do I get it out again?? I've tryed toothpicks but they got lost inside?? Also my computer is now making funny noises.

Belinda Y:

I don't know why some people have a problem with fox hunting. The foxes must enjoy it. Otherwise they wouldn't join in, would they?

Beth:

Damn! The power went out in the city. I got trapped on an escalator for hours!!!

Ray:

Do u mean u were stuck in an elevator or on an escalator?

Beth:

On an escalator.

Ray:

ok so y didn't u just walk dwn the escalator

Beth:

coz the power was out so it wasn't movin.

Ray:

But an escalator is made of steps.

Beth:

didn't think of that. lol

Pod:

Sumtime skool make me feel so dumb . . . :-(

Mindy:

Yipee! Just heard the news. I've got into collage:) :)

Carl:

Dear school plese cud u tel me why do u excist? yors suncerley me and about haf the dam world.

Lynda:

just had a phone call from raymon's school techer he says he wants to set up a meeting they have dun a teset on ray's eye q and found that it is extreemly high!!!!!! Thank you o lord!!!! We are blessed:)))))

Sheree:

At last finished my asignment. Misson ACOMPLISHED!!!

Fred:

Let's hope the misson wasn't a spelling asignment.

Merv:
Uneducated people is a turn off.

Suzanne:
Why is that people always seem to understand estimate my intelligents?!

Nehemiah:
My business is just starting and it will expand in a extremly rapid manner when people see how far ahead i have thoght ahead with this business people will thank im a genious.

Chris L:
Someone gave out my mobile number! Which of you gave out my mobile number! I'm going to kill whichever of you gave out my mobile number!

AndyJ:
Everyone knows your mobile number, dude. You put it on your profile.

Phill:

Someone help! This is just my luck. I just drove my car down to the shops, got out and left my keys locked inside. Now it's beginning to piss down. The window is open so it's going to drench the inside of the car. Can anyone pick me up and take me home to get my spare keys.

Don:

If the windows is open can't you just reach in to get the keys?

Phill:

Oh yeah! Sorry! Lol

Chantelle A:

[at the time of the 2012 Olympics]

i think i just heard some guy on the olympics just say they started 3000 years ago! how does that work? its only 2012 now?!

Emily B:

3000 years ago? wow! was anyone even alive then?

Jason M:

Does anyone know what brb means?

Nige B:

Be right back.

Jason M:

OK. So will you tell me what it means when you get back?

Observations to Leave You Speechless

Sometimes you can be really stupid without the assistance of anyone else. You don't have to be asked a daft question first; you can just leap out onto the Internet like some manically carefree skydiver without a parachute and, like him, fall flat on your face.

That's the great thing about the Internet: it's there all the time, so nothing can prevent you from sounding off at any time of day or night.

You've just got back from the pub, three sheets to the wind, and are stumbling around the house looking for the curry paste so you can make a nice sandwich when you spot the computer in the corner of the room with its cursor winking at you seductively.

I'll just do a bit of surfing, you think, eagerly getting that tactile mouse in your sweaty palm. Before you know it, you've been on the thing for an hour and a half and have posted messages to all and sundry. The common denominator of all these messages is that there's not an ounce of sense in any of them.

Back in the day, drunks stood on street corners shouting at passers-by, challenging lamp posts to fights and generally barking at the moon. Now, they stand on the cosmic street corner of the Internet and talk utter nonsense.

Oh, well, it's progress, I suppose.

Never forget – wrong was not built in a day.

I'm hoping the old saying is true. Time heals all wombs.

What I always say is you never really know who someone is until you know them.

Little things always make me ovary act.

Twitter is my alter eagle.

These days I only smoke healthy cigarettes.

If you really wanted, you could bite through your finger almost as easy as you could bite through a sausage. But then your brain pipes up and says, 'Hey, man! Biting off your finger is going to hurt.' And that is why people don't bite off their fingers.

Sleep is one of the best things you can do if you don't want to be awake.

Sometimes when I close my eyes, it's like I can't see at all.

Just saw *Iron Man 3* in 3d. Wow! I wish life was in 3d.

Do not forget – death is invegetable!!!

Alik:

Elevators do not break. They simply turn into stairs. Be the elevator, people. Adapt.

Kris:

Did you mean to say escalators just then?

Alik:

Escalators do not break. They simply turn into stairs. Be the escalator, people. Adapt.

Problems With Speling and Grammer

It's difficult when English isn't your first language. It's even more difficult when language isn't your first language. But what is everybody else's excuse?

Some Internet missives look like someone has just picked a load of random words out of a hat (possibly a back-to-front baseball cap) and chucked them at the computer screen, hoping for the best. The grammar is grotty, the spelling is sloppy and the punctuation is . . . well, non-existent.

If there had been an explosion in an alphabet soup factory the text being cleared up afterwards by the emergency services would probably make more sense than half the stuff out there in cyberspace.

It's bad enough when postings are from teenagers trying to look cool by not giving a damn about 'some random rules of English made up by adults' but when the message is from an adult applying for a job it's beyond the pale – wherever the pale may be.

Worse still if the job they're applying for is Head of English at a school where they will be training the next generation in how to speak gobbledegook as a first language.

If you're of a nervous disposition look away now, but for those of you with a stout heart, read 'em and weep.

Sheree:
Just to let you all know that today is International Litarecy Day!
Dave:
Thank you for that great start to International Literacy Day!

Lukas:
People are so uneducated these days. It makes me so mad when people don't know the difference between 'they're', 'their' and 'there' . . . Their really stupid.

Yaz:

Went out for a meal tonite and had an awesome seizure salad.

Leila:

Ther is only one thing I wanna be in life and that is to be sucksexful!!!

Aaron:

There, they're and their. These are three things you need to be able to spell right now that your in college.

Wozz:

My girlfren has gon n lef me so today ther is no 'I' in 'happyness'.

Charlene:

Aw! Bless!

Conor:

There is an 'i' in 'happiness' if you learn to spell it right, dick brain.

Tracey Ann:

Ther is nothing I love more than wachting *Bridget Jones* at the same time as raping my christmas pressants.

Chris G:

U r RAPING ur Christmas pressants?

Shane D:

Oh my God! What have you been doing to that puppy I bought you?

Lucy:

Baking today. Trying to use as many spoons and bowels as possible so's I can lick 'em all clean.

Jenny:

Ugh! You're going to lick out a bowel?

Lucy:

I love to stick my face right in a bowel and lick it all out so all the goo is in my hair and up my nose.

Matty:

In a bowel! In a bowel In a bowel!!!!!!!

Robby:

at the hospitel n my grandpa is still sick n i have to watch him f***in a man tonite is gonna suck.

Mason:

Hey robby, i think u at least need to put in a comma there.

Robby:

Dats f***ed up man my grandpa is already sick n the last thing he need is to be put in a comma f*** you man!

Terri:

My approach to life is this. I would rather be pissed off then pissed on.

Micah:

That can be arranged.

Hazza:

You really ought to do some research on the difference between 'then' and 'than'.

Digga:

Hey, everyone, I got three free periods this afternoon. I can do whatever I f***ing want. Excellent!! Gotta say – I really love f***ing college guys!!!!

Timbob:

Digga mate, either you need to learn to use a comma or that's one hell of an admission you just made.

The World of
Online Dating

The Internet has made life easier in so many ways. These days you can hop online and, with just a few clicks, find a replacement for anything in your house that is looking a bit tired, a bit worn out or which isn't working as well as it used to. Unfortunately, this might be your partner.

Online dating is a booming industry. It is worth billions of pounds and there are a number of dating websites to choose from. If you wish to advertise that you're looking for a partner you can post your details on match.com, eHarmony, Friend Finder, okcupid or, if you are on a budget, eBay.

Millions have signed up to these dating services and a surprisingly high percentage of them are single and not already in a relationship. Nevertheless they have decided to go online to look for love, or perhaps just to do a quick Internet search, much as you might for a new electric kettle, to see what's currently available, how much it's going to cost you and how far you're going to have to drive to get it.

Some may see online dating services as akin to price comparison websites but others recognize that they provide a valuable function. After all, many find it difficult these days to find true love by the traditional methods of hanging around in bars, getting drunk at the office party or begging random passers-by.

It's far easier to find someone online. Not only that but, once you're online, it's much easier to lie about your height, weight, age, bank balance and whether or not you have any hair.

On the other hand, many of those who use dating sites describe themselves with extraordinary and brutal honesty. Or could it just be brutal stupidity?

—ɯ—

Posted by Kris:

Overweight, not particularly good looking man late fifties. I enjoy reading, music, travel, long walks in the countryside and being naked in public places. Would like to meet similar.

Dating site questionnaire:

What is the first thing that people usually notice when they meet you?

Frank:

My appearance and my face.

Man:

There are two things I need right now – a blowjob and something to eat. Any ladies care to suggest how they could help a dude out?

Woman:

How about you take a hooker to Dunkin Donuts?

Posted by Lynsey:

Hey. Hope you don't mind me contacting you again. remember a few weeks ago when you had sex with me although you didn't really like me that much? Could you let me have the recipe for the meatloaf you made for dinner that night?

Dating site questionnaire:
What is the most personal thing to which you are willing to admit?
Jeremy:
The fact that I am a virgin.
Updated June 2013: Too late, ladies! Not any more!

Posted by Tom:
I really enjoyed our date. I thought you looked so sexy. when I looked at you it was almost like looking at myself in the mirror.

Dating site questionnaire:
What is the first thing that people usually notice when they meet you?
Henry:
My samurai sword.

Dating site questionnaire:

What do you like to do on a typical Friday night?

Geoff:

Some weeks I like to stay in, other weeks I like to go out instead.

Posted by Karl:

I am going to be straight with you. I am a highly sexed male. 320 lbs. By all accounts not good for much. What I'm looking for is a girl. Preferably a dirty little freak. If you've got a bit of attitude, I'll tolerate that – within reason. If you're on parole and covered in tattoos – that's not a problem. In fact go to the front of the queue. But do not ask me to go to pay to download pics of you. I look at enough pics. I need real flesh right now. I'm not much and I'm promising nothing.

Dating site questionnaire:

What is the most personal thing to which you are willing to admit?

Kevin:

I have never had sex with a boy or a man.

Dating site questionnaire:
What sort of person would you ideally like to meet?
Kevin:
Anyone who is not a boy or a man.

Dating site questionnaire:
What do you like to do on a typical Friday night?
Tina:
I like to pluck my pubic hair ready for the weekend.

Posted by Henrietta:
Dear men, I am a fat, social outcast and I am looking for the sort of guy who can love me for who and what I am. I am a professional single woman. I have no children. I live with my cat and dog. I have not had sex in over five years. The sort of men I am not interested in are as follows: married men, men in relationships, homosexual men, bi-sexual men, drug using men, alcoholic men, violent men and men who cannot keep it in their trousers.

Dating site questionnaire:

What do you like to do on a typical Friday night?

Martyn:

I sit and contemplate the terrible things that men do unto one another.

Dating site questionnaire:

What sorts of things do you like to talk about with friends?

Samuel:

What heaven will be like when we get there.

Posted by Kenny:

This is a message to the lovely woman I met in the toilet of Pizza World, Brompton High Street last Thursday.

You had strawberry blonde hair, were wearing a green jacket and were I believe slightly drunk. I was sitting in the toilet cubicle having a huge poop. I had forgotten to lock the door because I had been in quite a rush to get in there. I'm sorry you found me with my trousers down. That must have surprised you especially as I wasn't concerned that you had walked into my cubicle. But I will never forget your beautiful brown eyes (no pun intended). You slammed the cubicle door on me as I called out, 'Hey, lovely lady'. But all of us have to poop. You have seen me pooping and I feel that has moved our relationship to a very special level. I hope you feel the same way and will get in touch and that I didn't offend you with my odour. I had just had a chilli pizza special and it hadn't quite agreed with me.

Dating site questionnaire:
What is the most personal thing to which you are willing to admit?
Stigg:
That on March 23 1980 I was abducted by aliens who took me to Venus to meet Jesus.

Dating site questionnaire:

What is the most personal thing to which you are willing to admit?

Robert:

I like to wear an oven mitt when I masturbate to make myself feel like a lumberjack then when I ejaculate I yell out, 'TIMBER!!!'

Harrods It Ain't – Buying and Selling on the Internet

Once upon a time if you wanted to buy something you just went into a shop and bought it, end of. Nowadays of course we have the Internet, which is supposed to make our lives easier, but for some reason shopping is ten times more complicated.

You have to give feedback, rate your experience, share your views, etc., etc., when all you wanted was a new set of windscreen wipers or something equally mundane.

In the old days you weren't forced to stand outside Woolworths or wherever you had just shopped and tell everyone passing by that you would have given your shopping experience ten stars but the sales assistant was a bit snotty with you so you're deducting one star.

If you wanted to sell your old bicycle you put an ad in the local newsagent's window and it was all nice and simple. You didn't have to upload pictures of your boneshaker from every angle, give chapter and verse on the squeaky wheel, the go-faster stripes or the cubic capacity of the saddlebag.

While your item was up for sale you weren't required to answer endless queries about the exact meaning of the phrase 'as new', or whether the colour was as it looked in the photo, or if the cat sitting next to the bicycle in the picture was included.

Once you'd sold your item you didn't have to endure endless emails from the buyer, asking where his or her item was, enquiring if you were a rip-off merchant and threatening to report you to Bill Gates or whoever runs the Internet.

Internet buying – how did we ever manage without it?

Harold M (buyer):
Item was ok but then I got a virus from the seller's thank you email. Thanks a bunch, dick-wad!

Trixie Boo (seller):
Excellent buyer. Thanks for sending payment through ultra fast. Although you didn't actually buy anything from me whatever.

Suzy F (buyer):
I rate this seller very highly. Will ask him to have my babies.

Donger (buyer):
Im not easily impressed but im relly impressed keep up the good work.

Pat W (buyer):
How refreshing to see this seller offers prices that are like round figures not £3.98 or some such. Jeez that annoys me.

Thunk head (buyer):
Item said delivery 7–10 days then it came next day while I was out. Thanks ever so much for that. Two-mile trip to collection office!

SallyG (buyer):
Ok, I ordered something brakable but that doesn't mean it has to be broken when it arrives even if its free deliverry and I'm not paying you to be a packager.

Peeps (buyer):
I was going to leave you feedback, but have decided not to. Cos I have a life.

Todd H. (buyer):
Not quite awesome but close.

Bountiful (buyer):
Whats that roman saying about buyer beware? Take my word for it and beware or is it be aware. Anyways, watch out as this sller is a conn artist.

Terri W. (buyer):
This was the first time I've ever bought anything online and it will be the last . . . until the next time I suppose.

Davros Peenworthy (seller):
If you don't like my stuff what I'm selling don't you diss me online come and diss me to my face if yous big enuff!

Reviews from Hell – 1

Magazines used to employ people called reviewers, who would leaf through books, watch countless films and listen to music – basically, so we didn't have to. Their job was to sort the wheat from the chaff, whatever chaff is, and tell us what to avoid and sometimes what to rush out and buy.

Because these people had read thousands of books, watched millions of films and listened to container-loads of music, they probably knew something of what they were talking about.

No longer.

Nowadays everyone is a reviewer. Don't know what you're talking about? No problem. Can't spell? Ditto. Have only the most tenuous grip on reality? Bring it on!

Welcome to the reviewers from hell.

Every dummy who has downloaded a song, read the first two pages of one book in their entire lives and thinks that *Citizen Kane* was a seventies sitcom starring Robert Lindsay can now set themselves up as a cyber Will Self/Barry Norman/Nick Kent and rip your meisterwork to shreds.

Magazine reviews, of course, only had a shelf life of a month and were read by a limited number of people. Online reviews are there *for ever,* being read by millions of people, and will only disappear when the sun finally goes out and civilization ends.

Oh, but happy reading anyway!

—⁓—

Reviews from Hell: Movies and DVD Section

The Passion of the Christ (2004) (DVD)
Starring Jim Caviezel
Directed by Mel Gibson

I Adore Thee, O Jesus!

Review by Theophilus E:

This movie will never be replicated. This is the foretaste of things to come. Until that day when we recieve perpetual rest in the Lord we must have pacience. We can only pray to see what heaven will be like but it may soon come to past that the lamb of god will return at what hour we know not but we still have time to change, my friends. Listen to your soul and seek ye the truth that lies deep within your being. For to find peace with ones self is gratefful, thanks be to god fir He is love and it is by your faith that ye will be saved. Ten out of ten stars. Amen.

Very very poor packaging

Review by Nathan F:

Very poor package. No extras. Producers should have included something to lighten the mood after two hours of graphic scourging and crucifixion. But no blooper reel or nothing.

Not Really What I Wanted

Review by John H:

This was not really what I wanted as I had actually intended to order *A Passion For Angling*.

Titanic (1997) (DVD)

Directed by James Cameron

Starring Leonardo di Caprio, Kate Winslet

Thank God the Look Out Guy Fell Asleep!

Review by Marcie Q:

i am so happy the guy on the titanic who was meant to be looking for icebergs fell asleep. otherwise the ship would never have sunk and I would never have got to see this all time great movie.

Not true

Review by Gary W:

I don't believe it's really true cos how could someone be filming it when everyone else was like dead and begin drounded?

I Love You *Titanic*!

Review by Glenda T:

I LOVE YOU TITANIC SO VERY MUCH I WATCH YOUR MOVIE OVER 500 TIMES AND THINK IS VERRY VERRY SAD MOVIE I AM SHRER THE FRIST OFFICER MUREY THINKS IT SAD TOO I FELL VERRY VERRY UPSET BECAUSE IT SANK I LOVE YOU TITANICCCCCCC

It sinks and it stinks!!!

Review by Richey H:

Spoiler alert – the ship sinks and all the people drown. I for one could not wait for that to happen.

***The Complete Adventures of Harry Potter* Box Set (2012) (DVD)**

Starring Daniel Radcliffe, Emma Watson and Rupert Grint

Serious disappointment!

Review by Josh L:

I bought this in hopes that I might at least get to see hermione's tits but nothing! I mean seriously guys! we want some skin!!!

Boogie Nights **(1997) (DVD)**

Starring Mark Wahlberg, Julianne Moore, Burt Reynolds

Directed by Paul Thomas Anderson

Too much nude stuff going on

Review by Perry P:

In my own opinion there is way to much nudity in this movie i hate nudity and this was so bad i blew some chunks on the couch. if you don't like nudity this is a movie you should much stay away from. you might need a sick bag. This is the worst movie i ever saw.

Apollo 13 **(1995) (DVD)**

Directed by Ron Howard

Starring Tom Hanks, Kevin Bacon, Bill Paxton

Ruined for me

Review by Randy R:

This is a movie about three spacemen who go to the moon in a rocket but then they have a malfunction and they cannot land on the moon's surface.

But there simply is no proof that men have ever traveled to the moon. In reality no one has gone more than 400 miles into space. So this movie is science fiction and it is garbage.

And while we are on the subject, if no-one really went to the moon, what did NASA do with all the money they got from U.S. taxpayers? We know the answer. They faked the moon landings and then have been funding films like *Apollo 13* ever since to trick us into thinking they really went to the moon.

Ron Howard should be arrested for making this film. And so should Henry Winkler. Even though he wasn't in it.

Hocus Pocus **(1993) (DVD)**

Directed by Kenny Ortega

Starring Bette Midler, Sarah Jessica Parker

Un-witchable!

Review by Thora:

This is not what it's like being a witch in real life. It is a gift that some are given. It is not something you should take advantage of. And believe me, I know of that which I speak.

Sleeping Beauty **(1959) (DVD)**

Directed by Clyde Geronimi

Starring Mary Costa, Eleanor Audley, Verna Felton

A classic fairy tale ruined by Disneyfication . . .

Review by Jeff:

This is yet another Disney so called classic in which all the things that made the original great have been torn out. I'm talking about stuff like the adultery, the rape, the cannibalism etc.

The Punisher (1989) (DVD)
Directed by Mark Goldblatt
Starring Dolph Lundgren, Louis Gossett Jr

Too much human parts!
Review by Reno:
Too much blood and human parts coming out of the people in this film. Also the speaking is all in English which must be mistake? Someone told me it was good film but no offence it did not work out for me. But that is just my own personal opinion.

Brokeback Mountain
Directed by Ang Lee
Starring Heath Ledger, Jake Gyllenhaal

Appalled by the homosexuality
Review by Christine:
This is a disgusting movie. There were two men in it who were obsessed with each other's backsides. This is not fit for family viewing or for anyone viewing. In the end I had to burn my copy.

The Day After Tomorrow (2004) (DVD)
Directed by Roland Emmerich
Starring Dennis Quaid

Total fiction!!
Review by Jackson K:
Global warming is a total fiction put about by anti-libertarian Democrats. It ain't never gonna happen and for this reason, this movie sucks.

Hall Pass (2011) (DVD)
Directed by Peter and Bobby Farrelly
Starring Owen Wilson, Jason Sudeikis

We should all 'pass' on this one
Review by Dan:
I watched this DVD. I only laughed once. And that was when my brother farted

Reviews from Hell:
Books Department – Adult Fiction

War and Peace
Author: Leo Tolstoy

Review by Dennis C:

Total rubbish. Vastly over-rated. Forget what other people say; don't bother picking this garbage up.

Review by Giles F:

I read the first four or five pages of this book. Didn't understand the plot line so I gave up.

Jane Eyre
Author: Charlotte Brontë

Review by Ellie:

OMG! coud a book be any more boooring? You kidding me? I mean come on! The book is so rubish and if you like it, then fine, but this is my opinion and I hate Justin Bieber!

Oedipus Rex

Author: Sophocles

Review by Stewart:

This book stank so bad it was like a long, warm glass of rancid milk. Firstly, there was too much incest going on for me. Nobody likes that. Also it was totally unbelievable. The Sphinx went round asking people riddles and if they got it wrong they got eaten? Oh really??? And the sphinx's riddle is a stupid riddle. And as for the blind guy who sees the future, don't even get me started!

Review by Miles H:

This book is all about a man who is too stupid to realize he's got married to his own mum. If I married my own mum, I am I sure I would notice.

Review by Bruno M:

In my opinion this story lacked many things. Plot, characters, setting, conflict and a decent theme tune.

Review by Gordy:

I found this book really boring. Also I didn't like it when they were all having sex with their own family. That was nasty. I didn't really understand it. I don't want to ever have to read this book again or to read anything about it again. It was not interesting in the slightest. The book of Oedipus, I do not care for it . . .

Romeo and Juliet
Author: William Shakespeare
Review by Ronnie:

I have just finished reading this book and cannot see what all the fuss is about. I don't care what anyone says this story is a pile of old cak. Plus it's full of clichés and old stuff. I have seen this all done better so many times before.

1984
Author: George Orwell
Review by Nick R:

This is arguably the worst book I have ever read. I cannot understand why anybody would choose to read this garbage.

Review by Iggy H:

This book has nothing to do with the eighties that I remember. Doesn't do what it says on the tin!

Review by Pat M:

Worst science fiction I've ever read. This is supposed to be a prediction of the future. But 1984 was like twenty-nine years ago!?

Mrs Dalloway

Author: Virginia Woolf

Review by J. Huggins:

This book was written by a lesbian! I think that pretty much says all I have to say on the subject. I don't want to read about these kind of people. I simply don't approve.

Review by Mr Hitler:

Not only could I not stay awake long enough to read this book, I can't believe anyone could stay awake long enough to write it.

Review by Billy D:

The only good thing you can say about this 'literary' drivel is that the person responsible, Virginia Wolof, has been dead for quite some time now. Let us pray to the Lord that situation continues. THIS BOOK IS LESS FUN THAN HAVING ROOT CANAL!

Review by Tommo:

This has got to be the best book I ever read!!!!!
I'm kidding. It's shit.

Waiting For Godot

Author: Samuel Beckett

Review by Ed:

Spoiler alert! This Godot dude doesn't even turn up!

Review by Entwistle G:

The whole thing is just like two guys talking. What's that all about?

Bring Up the Bodies

Author: Hilary Mantel

Review by Barbara C:

I give this book 8 out of 10 stars but this rating does not have anything to do with my opinion of the book. I am only half way through reading the book and so have not this far performed an opinion of it. However, a friend highly recommended the book to me.

Review by Bill D:

I read this book on the plane and it made my flight fly by.

The Da Vinci Code

Author: Dan Brown

Review by Jimmy:

I don't like this book. None of it is true. I think it may just be a story someone's made up.

Review by Jamie R:

God this book is absolutely awful though once I had gott over the shock I read it from cover to cover.

Reviews from Hell:
Books Department – Non-Fiction

Solitary Fitness
Authors: Charles Bronson and Stephen Richards
Review by Patti C:
I didn't actually read this book. So I do not know how to give an accurate rating. So I'm not going to. Thank you.

How to Defend Yourself in 3 Seconds (or Less!)
Author: Phil Pierce
Review by Donald:
You could always use this book to hit someone with as I know all too well.

Being Jordan

Author: Katie Price

Review by Vicky S:

i am proud to say i have never read a book before but i had heard this was good so i made an effort and i was realy suprised and was hooked from page 1 bare in mind im not a book girl at all. i read it in under three weeks.

Review by Ted (retired meat packer):

Bought this by mistake. I was travelling to Jordan and needed a guidebook. My usual reading is military history but nevertheless this book has changed my life. I find Jordan an inspiration to us all and similar in so many ways to my own dear wife. Jordan would have had what it took to make it in the meat packing trade. Well, done girl. Keep on adopting children and writing these books. Presuming you did write this one. And despite what my fourteen year old daughter keeps telling people, I have not taken a shine to Ms Jordan just because she has enormous bazonkas.

The Holy Bible

Author: New International Version

Reviews:

Really shoddy – the paper was far too thin.

OK. But there's not enough good fights in it.

This is God's second novel after the Old Testament and it's qiute a improvement in my opinion.

Although the e-book version is free its a waste of memmory because its impossible to work wouldnt reccommend.

I couldn't relate to the main character. He seemed so full of himself.

God created all things so why couldn't he have come up with a typeface that was easier to read.

To be honest I preferred the film.

A Brief History of Time

Author: Stephen Hawking

Review by Mr Mann:

This has to be the stupidest book I have ever read. Although I didn't actually read it in the end cos the cover looked so dumb.

Reviews from Hell:
Books Department – Children's Section

Harry Potter and the Philosopher's Stone

Author: J. K. Rowling

Review by A Christian:

I do not consider this book suitable for children of any age! It is about a boy called Harry and his friends who are all wizards at an imagenery school called Hagwurts. An evil devil being has killed Harry Potter's parents and is trying to get Harry Potter. Harry does not know why. I do. It is because Harry is doing wizardy witch craft. You should not let any child see this book. If they do they will start doing wizardy witch craft. At the end of the book Harry and his friends are happy. They should not be happy because they do wizardy witch craft. They should all be killed like Harry Potter's parents. I am disgusted with JK Rowling and this book she has written. She is not a Christian. It is not a Christian book.

Cloudy With a Chance of Meatballs
Author: Judi Barrett
Review by Judy P:
Many reviews say this is a popular book with children. I beg to differ. The underlying premise of the work is about eating meat or carnism. It is therefore highly unsuitable for children who are being brought up as vegetarians or vegans and I cannot recommend it.

Moo, Baa, La La La!
Author: Sandra Boynton
Review by Lorna C:
This is a board book for small children with pictures of animals and the noises they make. Mostly it's fine but some of the noises are not accurate. For a start Ms Boynton has three singing pigs going 'La, La, La'?

Oh really? Is that the noise pigs make where Ms Boynton lives? They certainly don't do that in the farm near where I live. Took my little boy there the other day. He starts singing 'La La La' when he sees the pigs . . . all the other mothers are looking at me like my kid's deranged while their kids are 'oink-ing' and snorting away. Clearly my child is not as clever as their mastermind children who know the correct pig noises. So thanks, Ms Boynton . . . thanks a bunch!!!

The Complete Adventures of Curious George
Authors: Margret and H. A. Rey
Review by Derek M:
I read this book to my child but it is quite scary and now my child won't go back in his bedroom. I think he may need professional help. Also my wife has become depressed after looking at the pictures in the book because she thought the colours were quite cold. I liked it though.

The Story of Babar the Little Elephant

Author: Jean de Brunhoff

Review by John C:

My little boy hates this book. Every time I pick the book up my son starts yelling, 'No, no, no!' This book is probably OK. but it makes my son cry. So I don't really know what it's about. So i cannot really review it.

Fairy Tales of Hans Christian Andersen

Author: Hans Christian Andersen

Review by a dad:

In my opinion this is an extremely dangerous book for small children. We placed it on a book shelf above my son's bed. Then one night while I was reading to him from another book it fell on my head and caused a significant abrasion. I have written to the publishers to complain but of course they refuse to accept any responsibility. Bloody typical.

Alice's Adventures in Wonderland

Author: Lewis Carroll

Review by Victor:

This book is like it was written a hundred years ago. Every page is full of old time words. No-one has time for this now. Sorry to Lewis Carroll and all of the classic old books but that is true.

The Very Hungry Caterpillar

Author: Eric Carle

Review by Mr Campbell:

The illustrations in this book are beautiful but they accompany text which is based on scientific knowledge which could be highly misleading to a small child. A butterfly does not come from a cocoon. A moth comes from a cocoon. As any intelligent person will know when a butterfly caterpillar pupates, it does not form a cocoon by spinning silk. If you want to teach your child inaccurate science, then this is the book for you.

Reviews from Hell – 2

Reviews From Hell: Music Department

The Dark Side Of The Moon by Pink Floyd

Review by Jezza:

A mixture of sounds is combined to make this album.

Review by Bryan:

I have to say I am totally mistyfied by all the hype surrounding this album.

Review by Boz:

I like it but just not any of the songs.

Review by Simmo:

I bought this album because I like their stuff.

Black Sabbath's Greatest Hits

Review by Porky:

I bought this hoping for some new material, but I can't believe it. it turns out to be just covers of old Sabbath songs done again. Not only that they're all completely identical to the orignals from the seventies.

The Beatles 1967–1970

Sid O:

Really disappointed. I have heard every single one of these songs before.

Gary W:

In my humble opinion the beetles are realy over-rated.

Reviews from Hell: Toys Department

Family Party: 30 Great Games Obstacle Arcade

I was good all year and farther xmas gave me this uselss game the grafix are rubbish.

Pippa Bling Bling Urban Girl Fashion Doll

Encourages little girls to be whores
Review by Jason F:
This over sexy play doll has got to be a new low even for our femi-nazi dominated culture-free nation. This whorish mannequin says one thing. It tells impressionable children that being arrogant, shallow, slutty and superficial are all things to aspire to. Any mother who buys one of these monstrosities for their child should be thrown in jail and have her tubes tied.

Transformers: Revenge of the Fallen (Playstation 2 game)

Awesome!!
Review by Bruce G:
1 out of 10 stars
Great game!!! great app!!!! ... The reason I'm only giving it one star is cause I'm a dick.

Reviews from Hell:
Household Department

Dog Grooming Nail Clippers

I was sent a muppet toy instead of the clippers!
Review by Lucy P:

So bad! I opened the package but it was a muppet toy not the clippers! who will told me why? who will told me why? who will told me why? who will told me why?

Acqua Di Romeo Parfum Spray For Men

Smelling good!
Review by Chas J. S:

Mainly I use this on my genitals. That way when they open my pants the ladies know I mean business. It's good to let them have a huge whiff of sexy down there.

Anti-Allergy Nasal Spray 100 Doses £2.99
Review by Nicholas S:

Enjoyed this film (*A Short History of Violence*) when I saw it at the cinema. The acting is very good but as the title suggests it is quite violent

Good but a bit penisy looking

Review by Rene K:

These are good because the sound quality is quite powerful but the problem is the ear pieces look like penises. This makes me feel weird because it feels like I am sticking a pair of little rubber penises in my ears. And just to make things worse, one of them looks like it has a vein on it.

Super Shaves Alpha Oil – Mentholated

LOVE IT!!

Review by Suzzy G:

I gott this to shave my cooch and i was scared that it was gooing to give me really bad razor rash but it actually works better than anything else I've ever used, and I've tried pretty much everything AND the menthol gives me a nicely tingle.

Disposable Sickbags Multi-Pack

Does What It Says On The Tin!

Review by Reg M:

Nice collection of airline sickbags (over 140 in all) just £8.99. Possibly the best I've ever used.

Non-Latex Lubricated Condoms

Not Recommended!

Review by Loobie Loo:

To be honest these work fine. At least I don't think I've been knocked up just yet. But I'm not going to recommend them to anyone cos recommending a condom would just be weird.

Electric Sandwich Toaster

Potentially Lethal!
Review by Tony D:
This device is a danger to small children, pets, people who are forgetful like me and tea towels. It makes a good toasted sandwich but I left mine on for four hours by mistake. When I got back three of my best tea-towels had been burnt to cinders.

Nylon Closed-End Dress Zip

Now That's What I Call Zippy!
Review by Spinky:
Wow! This zip may be the zippiest zip I've ever bought. Thnx!

Reviews from Hell: Holidays

Yes, there was a sea view but you had to stand on a chair to see it.

The staff and the service was so bad I thought it was because it was Mexico but from what I heard it's not like it everywhere.

The holiday was good but the beach was too sandy.

We went to Majorca and the cab drivers couldn't understand us as they were all Spanish.

I got so fed up with cleaning staff knocking on door I asked for a 'No molester' sign to hang on my knob.

Topless sunbathing on the beach should not be allowed. Our holiday was ruined because my husband had an accident while looking at another woman.

The hotel was quite hygienic apart from the restaurant.

How can all their shops close for 'siesta' when it's like the middle of the afternoon?

Mumbai was alright but everywhere you went it was spicy food and I don't even like spicy food.

It really should be explained in the brochure that there are fish in the sea because if you've got young children they could be scared.

Our hotel was miles from the beach – and that's even further in kilometers.

I couldn't believe it! The hotel was full of British tourists! The one reason we go abroad is to get away from these people!

Apparently the seafood in the hotel restaurant came straight out of the sea – absolutely disgusting!

There was a terrible smell all the time at this hotel but I would consider going back.

We were forced to queue outside where there wasn't even any air conditioning.

Terrible room. I had to plug my hairdryer straight into mains!

You should be aware there is a semens mission next door to this hotel.

Cheap and cheerful though not very cheerful thinking about it.

Shocked at how many stairs we had to climb to get to our room as they said there was a lift in their assets.

The Great Wall of China is worth a look but what's the point of it?

I'm pretty sure the sky shown in your brouchure was bluer than in real life. Dissapointing.

Really terrible. The local shops didn't stock any proper food like ginger nuts or cocoa pops.

This is a terrible hotel to hold a wedding at. this was absolutely the worst experience of my life. apart from marrying my wife obviously.

I booked a two bed room for my boyfriend and myself but was given a double room. I have been informed this morning by my doctor that I am pregnant. I hold you personally responsible for this. This would never have happened if you had given us the correct number of beds I asked for.

That is the last St Patrick's night I spend in Greece! They don't know a thing about it. Never even heard of Irish coffee!

When arriving at this resort we weren't even offered a drink. I didn't want a drink but nevertheless . . .

Awful smell at this hotel like roar sewidge.

We had to find alternative accomodation because when we got there we found our hotel was water flooded!

Room overlooked the louts garden which was beautiful.

Your brochure states: 'No hairdressers at the accommodation'. My boyfriend and I are both trainee hairdressers. Will we have to stay somewhere else?

Reviews from Hell: Pubs and Restaurants

The restaurant had got a real nice umbeyonce.

Went to this pub on Tuesday, Wednesday and Friday last week. If your looking for a place with a good atmosphere and a good selction of beers drinks avoid this place.

This is the worst pub I have been in for years which in my book rates it pretty low.

Decent pub, even a lot of the graffiti is quite 'clean'.

If inspector morse was real this is the sort of pub he'd drink in or theragain maybe he wouldn't.

This pub should have been closed down years ago and if it had of been I wouldn't of gone there.

This meal was supposed to come with vegetables but instead it was peas!

After the meal I had chronic diarrea and vomiting too boot.

I checked all the reviews before I went and they were absolutely right – it was terrible.

Several tables at this pub had 'reserved' signs on them but there was no one sitting there – what's the point?

The flies seemed to like the food more than we did.

Waiter, there are flies in my soup

This meal was dreadful and luckily for me didn't taste of anything.